SAVAGE STRATEGIES FOR WINNING BIG IN BUSINESS & IN LIFE!

HUNT IT DOWN KILL IT & DRAG IT HOME

SAVAGE STRATEGIES FOR WINNING BIG IN BUSINESS & IN LIFE!

HUNT IT DOWN KILL IT & DRAG IT HOME

DAVID THOMAS ROBERTS
AWARD-WINNING BESTSELLING AUTHOR

Keynote BOOKS

RENEGADE CAPITALIST
Book Series

Hunt It Down Kill It & Drag It Home™

Copyright © 2022 David Thomas Roberts

First Edition: 2022

Printed in the United States of America

10 9 8 7 6 5 4 3 2 1

All rights reserved. No part of this publication may be reproduced, distributed, or transmitted in any form or by any means, including photocopying, recording, or other electronic or mechanical methods, without the prior written permission of the publisher, except in the case of brief quotations embodied in critical reviews and certain other noncommercial uses permitted by copyright law.

This book is a work of non-fiction. The author has made every effort to ensure that the accuracy of the information in this book was correct at time of publication. Neither the author nor the publisher nor any other person(s) associated with this book may be held liable for any damages that may result from any of the ideas made by the author in this book.

Published by Keynote Books

Keynote BOOKS

An imprint of Defiance Press & Publishing, LLC

DEFIANCE PRESS & PUBLISHING

ISBN-13: 978-1-955937-03-0 (Paperback)
ISBN-13: 978-1-955937-53-5 (eBook)
ISBN-13: 978-1-955937-54-2 (Hardcover)

Also available in audiobook format on Audible©

Printed in the USA by Defiance Press

Published by Keynote Bookes, An imprint of Defiance Press and Publishing, LLC
Bulk orders of this book may be obtained by contacting Defiance Press and Publishing, LLC at: www.defiancepress.com.

Public Relations Dept. – Defiance Press & Publishing, LLC
281-581-9300
pr@defiancepress.com

Defiance Press & Publishing, LLC
281-581-9300
info@defiancepress.com

DEDICATION

This book is dedicated to the Savages who, with an indominable spirit, have ventured regardless of risk and have experienced failures and disappointments while putting up with naysayers, government incompetence and corruption and yet have found a way to hunt it down, kill it, and drag it home every single day for the benefit of their tribe.

TABLE OF CONTENTS

Dedication..5
Prologue..9
Lesson 1: The Peasant 17
Lesson 2: The Aristocrat....................................25
Lesson 3: The Savage...29
Lesson 4: A Savage Built That 37
Lesson 5: Savage Vision....................................41
Lesson 6: Savage Habits 45
Lesson 7: Savage Problem-Solving.................51
Lesson 8: Savage Relationships 55
Lesson 9: Savage Warfare 61
Lesson 10: Savage Persistence.........................65
Epilogue..69

PROLOGUE

Yes, you *can* have it all.

But only if you become a *Savage*.

There it is. *I said it.*

I would be the first to agree that 'having it all' means different things to different people. For many, finding the love of your life and the enduring love of a family is enough. For others, having enough money to live comfortably and having the respect of loved ones, colleagues and friends is invaluable. Having a relationship with your God could be another. And of course, having your health cannot be underrated.

If you were to ask most people what it means to 'have it all', chances are most would leave out the one thing that true *Savages* possess that gives true meaning to the other features listed above.

Most would leave it out because most do not consider it achievable. We will get to that in short order.

You can apply *Savage* principals in all areas of your life, but few understand what it really takes to become a *Savage*.

And fewer know what a *Savage* actually is.

A *Savage* is self-made.

Savages are completely self-reliant.

Savages can seem like stubborn brutes.

Savages can forgive, but they never forget.

Savages are likely never politically-correct or 'woke'.

Savages generally don't care what others think.

Savages will defend their families and their tribes to the death.

Savages don't wallow in self-pity.

Savages distrust any authority meted out by *Aristocrats*.

Savages empathize with *Peasants*, but they don't enable them.

It's doubtful *Savages* are born with all of these traits when coming out of the womb. More than likely, a *Savage* interacts with his or her environment, including the influences where these instincts are cultivated—whether by family or whether some are fortunate enough to have had a mentor or a real *Savage* influence in their life.

Savages are the patriarchs and matriarchs of their families. Tribes survive generationally because of *Savage* leadership. *Savages* practice tough love even today, in an era of soft cultural mayhem.

Savages have heart in terms of bravery and their ability to give and receive love.

But don't expect me or any other *Savage* to accept mediocrity, small thinking, or a defeatist attitude. We simply cannot relate to it. *Savages* never utter the phrase, *"Woe is me"* even in their own personal self-talk.

Do *Savages* have problems, and is their life perfect? Of course they have problems, as they too have challenges in life, and their existence is certainly not without speed bumps along the way. But *Savages* react to these challenges differently than the rest of society.

Savages relentlessly attack their problems until they are solved. *Savages* never lose. If they are beaten, it's only temporary.

Savages never let their problems define them. *Savages* learn to be problem-solvers. *Savages* become proficient at identifying the root cause and by taking decisive action.

Savages are defined by their relentless persistence to *never quit!*

Savages ruthlessly protect themselves from negative people. *Savages* run from negative influences as if avoiding the plague. The same goes for *any* negative influence in your life including a negative family member, customer, associate, employee or vendor. A negative influence in your life will severely drain you of *Savage* mental capital—and you simply can't afford it. Nobody can. One cannot underestimate the destructive power of negative energy. Love those negative folks, but love them from a distance.

PROLOGUE

Savages don't make excuses.

The minute anyone accepts their own excuses for not achieving their maximum life potential—that is their guarantee of a life of mediocrity. In other words, they voluntarily become a permanent member of the *Peasant* class!

Peasants have a plethora of excuses to fall back on:

- I came from a broken family.
- I'm not college educated.
- I'm too old.
- I'm too young.
- I've got dyslexia.
- I'm not a salesperson.
- I'm afraid of rejection.
- I'm a minority.
- I'm not attractive.
- I'm overweight.
- I've got a medical condition.
- I have a learning disability.
- I'm not a good conversationalist.

- I'm broke.
- I fear failure.
- I fear success.
- My spouse won't let me.
- I don't want to pay higher taxes.
- My finances are in terrible condition.
- I have too much debt.
- My family won't support me.
- I don't like risk.
- I'm comfortable.
- I lack training.
- It's my boss's, colleague's, family's (fill in the blank) fault.

Do these excuses sound familiar?

Personally speaking, I could have easily used several of those excuses to shrink from my *Savage* pursuit. The truth is, for a *Savage,* the list above stokes *Savage* fire by becoming *reasons* and not excuses.

I love it when someone says, "You can't . . ." A *Savage* lives to hear those words.

Savages do not have contempt for *Peasants.*

The same cannot be said for *Savages'* contempt of *Aristocrats*. In fact *Savages* have genuine empathy for the plight of *Peasants*. *Savages* know that a *Peasant* has it within their power to change their circumstances and their tribe.

Earlier in this Prologue I mentioned what it means to 'have it all' and that most people will claim some of the same things already mentioned like money, health, respect and love. But they forget the one main ingredient and motivator for a *Savage*.

FREEDOM.

Savage freedom is waking up each morning knowing that you don't have to report anywhere or—more importantly—to anybody!

I hope this book leads you on your *Savage* quest and your ultimate fight for your *SAVAGE FREEDOM!*

Be a *Savage!*

LESSON 1

THE PEASANT

Peasant **(noun)**

    peas - ant \ pe-zent

    Definition of a Peasant:

    1. Usually an uneducated person or a person of low financial means or social status.

    2. Original use in Europe: a coarse, unsophisticated, or boorish person. Typically a term reserved for laborers.

Beware! *Peasant*s of every tribe are taught to "go get a good education" (typically provided by the government); then go out and get a "good" job. The minute a *Savage* begins to think for themselves and proclaim that sitting in a cubicle and working for the *Aristocrats* is not for them, other *Peasants* try to discourage them. Some of these *Peasants* could likely be your family, close friends and colleagues, or society in general.

Don't be a *Peasant*.

Be a *Savage*.

The average *Peasant* feels entitled, demanding basic necessities and even luxuries as a *right*. God forbid, a *Peasant* might have to take a risk to improve their life. *Peasants* develop habits that reinforce the status of *Peasants* their entire lives. *Peasants* are threatened by any fellow *Peasant* who wants to lift their head and stand among the *Savages*. It's like the saga of the crabs in the bucket . . . the crabs rarely escape because they keep getting pulled back by their fellow crabs.

Let's face it. The average *Peasant* is living paycheck to paycheck, waiting for their next three-day vacation and wasting their entire Sunday watching the gladiators of the day, making millions in government-funded stadiums while they disrespect our country all along the way. That weekend game is the highlight of a *Peasant's* week. A typical *Peasant* is wrapped up in a sports team where their self-worth is contingent upon winning Sunday's game. The Peasant will spend exponentially more time on this obsession than working on themselves to be able to make more money for their family or tribe—if they spend money at all.

Peasants don't take risks. That's one of the main reasons why they remain *Peasants*.

Most *Peasants* don't believe they are *Peasants*. Of course, a *Peasant* isn't always dirt poor. But Peasants, generally, are never *free*. The middle class is full of *Peasants*.

Peasants and *Aristocrats* have a symbiotic existence as they depend on each other to make the current system work. *Peasants* keep voting for *Aristocrats* who promise to improve their lives by taking more from the *Savages* and giving it to the *Peasants*. This continues to be true despite decades of proof that the *Aristocrats* generally are only interested in their own status in society and at the expense of the *Peasants*. *Aristocrats* continually rob from the goose who laid the golden egg (*Savages*) with no regard for the dynamics of capitalism and our Founders' value on liberty.

The current state of the *Peasant* can be attributed to the progressive ideology of the *Aristocrat's* education system over the last one hundred years. Today's *Peasant* children don't learn financial literacy, business, history or civics. Without those tools, the likelihood of a *Peasant* becoming a *Savage* is remote.

Aristocrats have allowed *Peasants* to become hopelessly indebted in an education that is essentially worthless or whose ROI (return on investment) may take twenty years or more. Today's *Peasant* class is another lesson in slavery.

Throughout history, the *Peasant* class has more health problems, a lower standard of living, a shorter life expectancy, higher disease rates and more mental health issues. The *Peasant* tribe is not self-sustaining and has little or no regard for the overall improvement of their fellow tribes.

Peasants are taught and have accepted that all accumulation of wealth of any kind is a zero-sum game, meaning that if they personally have less, it's because the *Savages* have more, or the *Savages* have stolen it from them. The *Peasants* have the *Aristocrats* to thank for fostering this belief system in their fellow tribes.

Peasants allow others to control their time, their income, their vacations, their commute and where they live. Get on any major freeway in a major city in the USA on a Monday morning and see the lemmings a.k.a. *Peasants* fighting traffic to go to a job they hate, reporting to a boss for whom they have no respect and for less money than they want to make. This is a premiere example of living a life of quiet desperation.

Most *Peasants* are literally weeks or even days away from financial ruin. Losing a job and the accompanying paycheck for several weeks for most would lead to disaster. This is paycheck prison. The *Peasant* is locked into a lifestyle (debt) they can't afford; therefore they become very risk adverse to any ideas where they could break free from this prison.

Peasants live for vacations and the weekends. TGIF (thank God it's Friday) is a real phenomenon to a *Peasant*.

Peasants allow change to dictate their lives. Most *Peasants* live their lives like a pinball machine. They bounce from one financial crisis to the next. Rather than adapt to change, the *Peasant* becomes a victim of their own lack of vision, keeping them from identifying how to adapt. The

Peasants—aided by Aristocrats' stagnant programs—allow life-changing opportunities to pass them by. Their tribe's standing in life does not change.

All *Peasants* are not created equal. Make no mistake; there are different levels and scales associated with *Peasants* ranging from the very poor who live in squalor to the highest level of *Peasant*. That fact may surprise you. Yes, there are business owners who fall into this category. Take for example a dentist, who is saddled with college tuition loans and loans for dental equipment to open a practice. They have payroll and other expenses. The dentist trades his/her time and labor for money. If the dentist doesn't practice his/her trade, he or she has no income. The dentist is a prisoner to his own practice. Does the dentist have *Savage* freedom? Probably not. Can the dentist walk away from his or her practice for two months and travel Europe and expect their income to remain the same? Again, probably not.

Although the dentist may have a higher income than the minimum-wage-earning *Peasant* who works in a fast food restaurant, the principles of debt, income and freedom remain the same. Do they have different castes in society because of who they are? Yes, unfortunately, that is a facet of our society in general This is despite the fact that it's entirely possible the personal balance sheet of a fast food worker with zero debt could in fact be more solvent than the dentist who has a ton of debt. One could also argue the fast food worker doesn't have the added stress of the debt that causes the dentist to experience sleepless nights.

The great news for both is that by applying *Savage* strategies to their circumstances, each has the ability to become a *Savage*. But it will involve changing how they think about almost everything!

Don't be a *Peasant*.

Be a *Savage*.

LESSON 2

THE ARISTOCRAT

Aristocrat **(noun)**

A-ris-to-crat

Definition of an Aristocrat:

1. A member of the aristocracy (ruling class) or people in real or an imagined rank in a community or society, a noble, an elite.

2. One who favors an aristocracy as a form of government.

3. Anything regarded as the best, most elegant or stylish of its kind by a small group of people.

Nothing remains the same. Not in the environment. Not in business. Not in life.

Savages generally have deep contempt for *Aristocrats*. This is principally because of the outward disdain exhibited by *Aristocrats* to any self-made *Savage*, who try to limit them, regulate them, govern them and rob them (taxes).

The *Savages* are responsible for the seismic change that has happened throughout history—from the Industrial Revolution to the Digital Age. *Savage* successes redefine industries, technology, medicine and business.

This has always been true. And the *Aristocrats* simply hate that fact.

Aristocrats are always a step behind, as they try to figure out how to capitalize from the changes made by *Savages* so as to manipulate a tax code, regulation or other calamity in an effort to milk resources from the *Savage* to give to the *Peasant* in exchange for their vote. This cycle keeps *Aristocrats* in positions of power.

Aristocrats are slaves to status, prestige and perception. Many Aristocrats outwardly appear to be men or women of means, but don't be fooled. *Aristocrats* place emphasis on *appearing* wealthy, but in reality, they have financed their cars, home, education and lifestyle to a point where each *Aristocrat* is really a *Peasant* with more social status. *Savages* in Texas refer to Aristocrats as "all hat and no cattle."

Aristocrats always take credit for the *Savages*' seismic changes when they benefit *the Aristocrats*. *Aristocrats* are only innovative in their schemes to extract from *Savages* when riding the wave of successes that *Savages* continually produce.

The *Peasants* who remained behind as the *Savages* found better ways to hunt and gather food either lived a substandard existence or starved to death. Stubborn in their ability to accept change and adapt, they believe what the *Aristocrats* always tell them that it's not their fault for being *Peasants* because the *Savages* take unfair advantage.

Aristocrats are the parasites on society cloaked as statesmen politicians, bureaucrats and government employees. They see it as their birthright to invoke regulations on the *Savages* and to dole out the left-over crumbs to the *Peasants*.

Aristocrats rarely live by their own rules; instead they force archaic laws and regulations on the masses but exempt themselves. Some *Aristocrats* play the part so well and yet, somehow, they become wealthy on government salaries.

An *Aristocrat* never creates anything on their own. How well they learn to manipulate their parasitic existence determines how high on the *Aristocrat's* totem pole they climb.

Can an *Aristocrat* become a *Savage*? Certainly, but it is rare. Does a *Savage* ever become an

Aristocrat? Yes, that can happen. The perfect example is Donald Trump. But that is also a good example of the fact that *Savage* traits aren't easily unlearned. Those *Savage* traits deeply-rooted in Trump simply sent the Washington, DC *Aristocrats* into frenzied hysteria that has led to countless investigations, hearings and wasted resources that continue to this day.

Aristocrats believe their ability to compromise makes them *noble*. Can the *Savage* compromise? Of course, they can, but not on the principals that founded their *Savage* core being; nor can they compromise on the health, safety and enduring legacy of their tribe. Nothing brings more contempt from a *Savage* than the pompous *Aristocrat*.

An *Aristocrat* has no idea how to *Hunt It Down, Kill It, and Drag it Home!*

Don't be an *Aristocrat*.

Be a *Savage*.

LESSON 3

THE SAVAGE

Savage **(noun)**
> Definition of savage:
>
> 1. Usually an uneducated person or a person of low financial means or social status.
>
> 2. Original use in Europe: a coarse, unsophisticated, or boorish person typically reserved for laborers.

Is a *Savage* born, or made?

Throughout our history, humans have had to adapt, and they had to become *Savage*s to survive. The weak rarely survived for long. So, no matter what personality type you were born with, God gave each of us an instinct to survive no matter what.

But God also embedded in each of us the instinct to *excel*!

A S*avage* doesn't use their personality as an excuse. What would a *Savage* say to his hungry family who expect to eat, or what would he say to his tribe when he arrives empty handed back at the cave from a long day of hunting?

Throughout history a family unit or a village of family units (a tribe) were dependent on their brave *Savage* warriors to *Hunt It Down, Kill It, and Drag It Home*!

Over the eons, with the evolution of industry and technology (both developed by *Savages* throughout history), no longer do humans have to survive by shear brawn or force. The brute *Savages* in history who have taken risks have elevated the human race and thus made it possible for government *Aristocrats* to take care of the masses and for the average *Peasant* to hold onto a job and hammer out a hand-to-mouth existence.

If not for the *Savages*, there is no funding of governments (thus no welfare), no innovation, no inventions, no capital, no cures for disease and not many of the comforts of life we have come to expect and which both *Peasants* and *Aristocrats* feel is their birthright.

It is the *Savages* that are responsible for the seismic change that has happened throughout history from the Industrial Revolution to the Digital Age. *Savage* successes redefine industries, technology, medicine and business.

Prehistoric *Savages* had to take risks every day. Hunting for food or establishing a territory for the tribe wasn't an effort in negotiation. Today, most *Peasants* are conveniently detached from the process that landed the slab of meat in the store for their easy consumption. There probably is not much thought put into the fact that *Savages* raised the herd; *Savages* started and built the meat processing plant; a *Savage* started a trucking company and a *Savage* created the grocery store chain that made life so easy for the *Peasant* that he/she didn't even have to be a part of the dirty work that resulted in their slab of beef making it to their kitchen in a nicely wrapped cellophane package. The average *Peasant* is far removed from the bloody task necessary to provide their next steak or their chicken dinner.

Are all wealthy individuals *Savages*?

No. It would certainly be determined by *how* they got wealthy. Was it inherited? Did they climb the corporate ladder?

A *Savage* is simply self-made. Period.

Is a CEO who has made millions in stock options a *Savage*? No, that CEO is an *Aristocrat*. If the CEO didn't start the company themself or take the risks of taking their ideas to market, then they were able to capitalize on the genius of the *Savage* that started the firm.

The first lesson in becoming a *Savage* is to learn to calculate and manage risk. It's literally impossible to become a *Savage* without willingness to take risks. A *Savage*, however, doesn't take reckless risks.

In order to bring food home to his family, a *Savage* must gauge whether to walk across that thin log that spans a 200-foot gorge to get to more fertile hunting ground on the other side. The *Savage* must take risks with his hunting weapon of choice, a bow for instance to shoot from a distance or a spear which may be deadlier but requires that the *Savage* get closer to his prey—or possibly even *become* the prey.

A *Savage* realizes that they may not be successful

in their daily hunt, but the thought of becoming a *Peasant* begging for scraps from the *Aristocrats* is never an option. While a *Savage* may not snag his prey today, there is eternal optimism in tomorrow, and the *Savage* will always prepare for tomorrow's success.

The wisdom of *Savages* is grounded in their spiritual being and in the legacy and pride of their tribe. Compromise is only possible if such decisions do not violate the very ethos of their being. A *Savage* is grounded, no matter how large his tribe is or how successful a *Savage* he or she has become. This is because the *Savage* has an endearing cause in their DNA that simply can't be altered or erased, even under the most difficult circumstances.

Highly underrated is the ability of the *Savage* to listen to members of their tribe and to consider those voices when leading. Is a *Savage* always loved by 100 percent of their tribe? No. But a true *Savage* has the respect of his or her entire tribe despite differences in the tribe's leadership.

Savages are human, and they do make mistakes. A *Savage* can lose his designation as a *Savage* with repeated transgressions against God's laws. When these transgressions become prevalent, a *Savage* can lose respect within their tribe, or their family and thus will invite the enemy to take advantage of their weakness.

Savages are not uncaring to the young, the elderly or to the weak who cannot fend for themselves. *Savages* honor their parents, especially later in life, and they regularly tap into the wisdom that has been gained by their long lives on earth. Experience can be a masterful teacher and this is not lost on the *Savage*.

Savages study finances and are astute in financial literacy. *Savages* never spend more than 80 percent of their income on living expenses. A *Savage* avoids debt and never finances luxuries.

Take away the trappings of success from a *Savage*, including wealth, property and their toys, and a true *Savage* will eventually find themself right back in the same place of success.

Why?

Because a *Savage* has learned how to *"Hunt It Down, Kill It, and Drag It Home."*

LESSON 3

Don't be a *Peasant*.

Don't be an *Aristocrat*.

Be a *Savage*.

LESSON 4

A SAVAGE BUILT THAT

Throughout history, major advances in almost every category of business, technology and medicine are the direct result of the vision and efforts of the *Savage*.

The debate stirred by President Obama in his second term in office about who really built "that" is ludicrous on its face. Obama claimed that the *Savage* couldn't have built "that" without the roads, infrastructure, etc. provided by the government. It's the classic chicken-versus-egg debate.

Except, it's not really a debate at all.

The infrastructure wouldn't exist without the

taxes generated by the blood, sweat and tears of the *Savages*.

Proof?

What came first, the *Savage* or the government infrastructure? The *Savages* were plying his/her trades long before there were governments.

Savages didn't need a government to feed and clothe the children of their tribes. They didn't need a government to erect their huts, to make their weapons, to store their food, to teach their children, etc.

Aristocrats on the other hand depend on the production of *Savages* to fund government. Even today, *Savage* income taxes make up the vast majority of government revenue, despite the fact that *Aristocrats* attempt to demonize the *Savages* to win the *Peasant* vote.

Savages win consistently and are deeply competitive. *Savages* succeed despite the regulations, roadblocks and bureaucracies put in front of them by the *Aristocrats*.

More tools exist today than ever in human history, and those tools allow *Savages* to exceed. But there are also impediments that our *Savage* ancestors never had—and most of those can be directly related to the efforts by *Aristocrats* to manage *Savages*.

A *Savage* cannot be managed in the traditional sense. Whenever the shackles of regulation and persecution are minimized, *Savages* change the world.

The masses can thank a *Savage* for nearly every facet of the conveniences they enjoy in daily life, for the advances in technology, manufacturing, medicine and the arts.

America was built by *Savages* who understood that freedom was the single most important achievement a *Savage* could accomplish. *Savages* risked everything to gain freedom from the *Aristocrats* of England, and they succeeded.

Did *Savages* build that business? Did they build America?

You bet they did.

Be a *Savage*.

LESSON 5

SAVAGE VISION

A *Savage* is a visionary. *Peasants* are not. *Aristocrats* are not.

Vision, in this context is not 20/20. *Vision* is the ability to see what isn't there—but *could* be.

The most successful *Savages* in history had particularly keen vision and absolute belief in the vision they formed. This is true from the *Savage* who sat by the campfire telling his tribe that the land over the mountains would be fertile hunting ground, to the *Savage* entrepreneur with his vision of a gadget that could be the *next big thing*.

In rare cases, some *Aristocrats* have had the ability to expand upon the original vision that the *Savage* created, long after the creator was gone. Never forget, however, that opportunity never existed without the original *Savage*. Companies that have continued to produce new products and technology innovations have only succeeded as they allowed *Aristocrats* an opportunity to act like a *Savage* with the risk removed.

The engineer who designs a new and successful product had that vision regardless of being employed by the *Aristocrat*, but the engineer was not able or willing to accept the risk of doing it themselves and building their own tribe.

There will always be *Peasants*. They are needed to carry out the vision of the *Savage*. *Aristocrats* need *Peasants* in order to establish their superiority in the social pecking order. There will always be *Aristocrats* who ride the wave created by the *Savages*.

The *Savage* has developed the ability to turn an idea or vision into a game plan which they execute.

Aristocrats have policies. *Peasants* have no

vision, and they rarely look past the next paycheck or three-day vacation and they waste their God-given time watching their favorite sports team.

Savages constantly work on their ideas. *Peasants* watch professional football on television and mow their own lawns. *Aristocrats* have policy and planning meetings.

Savages have a vision of what could be and spend every waking hour making it a reality for themselves and their tribes.

Get *Savage* vision.

Be a *Savage*.

LESSON 6
SAVAGE HABITS

Everyone has daily habits that make each person a *Peasant*, an *Aristocrat* or a *Savage*. A *Savage* is the sum of their habits, just as it is for *Peasants* and *Aristocrats*. The difference in those daily habits may not be easily discernable without examining them.

A *Peasant* and an *Aristocrat* allow themselves to fall into a similar habit, which grows into a resistance to changing those habits that could make them *Savages*. A *Savage* is constantly aware of his or her habits and monitors those habits to make sure they are carrying themselves and their tribe toward their vision.

Peasants do things the same way every day because they cannot accept the risk of making changes. After all, change is hard. *Aristocrats* encourage *Peasants* to keep doing the things that keep *Aristocrats* in power, which is basically doing the same things that created *Peasants* in the first place. *Savages* continually ask themselves if a certain task or use of their time is going to help them win at business and in life.

Savages continually sharpen their tools for winning, always looking for ways to improve themselves and the tools they use in their daily *Savage* chores. *Peasants* are always looking for the easy way out, the quickest way to relax or avoid the sacrifices *Savages* make to rise closer to the top of the food chain. Eventually, *Peasants'* inner *Savage* flame is crushed by the years that fly by, never altering course and changing habits in the slightest to improve their lot or the lot of the tribe.

Aristocrats are not much different, except for the fact that they create habits that enable them to rule over and take advantage of *Peasants*. *Aristocrats* have habits that allow them to *feel* or *appear* like *Savages*, but an *Aristocrat* never becomes a *Savage*. *Aristocrats* have a vested interest in keeping *Peasants* where they are by promising them the redistribution of the *Savages'* labor.

Savages wake up each day with a plan, and work daily on executing that plan. *Peasants* have no plan, and live their lives managing financial, family and spiritual drama.

Savages are never defined by the urgency of the moment, although *Savages* find ways to brilliantly get through the fog of any difficult circumstance. *Savages* operate on their own system of daily, weekly and monthly habits that they have identified as being critical to his/her success. In the course of human history, these *Savage's* habits were critical for their own survival and the survival of their tribe.

How does a *Savage* ensure that his tribe doesn't freeze to death in the winter? *Savages* gather and cut wood daily, never allowing themselves to be caught in severe weather without the ability to warm the tribe. Firewood could be synonymous with cash resources for the modern-day *Savage*. Saving for a rainy (or freezing) day is the *Savage* way. No matter how good the bounty of the moment, there will always be a circumstance where that stash of cash will come in handy—or even become life-saving.

Modern-day *Savages* scout for new leads, prospects, opportunities and customers as their ancestors scouted for new game and potable water.

Savages don't 'burn daylight' by wastefully sleeping in. They wake early to the new challenges of the day.

A *Savage* spends a few minutes a day in deep meditation, visualizing the tasks at hand and putting themselves in winning situations in their mind's eye.

Modern-day *Savages* keep their bodies and minds in peak condition, eating correctly, exercising and reading.

Savages have no time to spend with those who are critical or bring them down. They keep their swords sharp, realizing '*steel sharpens steel*' and only commiserating with those who can help them improve their hunting skills.

Savages identify the tasks that produce the most results and delegate tasks that can be done by others so as to operate at the peak efficiency of their talents.

Savages understand the wisdom of listening, using their ears more than their mouths.

Savages are highly punctual and demand the same from others, especially those in their tribe.

Savages do not participate in gossip or innuendo, as those are the habits of *Peasants* and *Aristocrats*.

Savages learn and practice the habit of continually giving credit to others, knowing that respect is only earned when making others feel better about themselves simply by practicing genuine empathy and sincere edification.

Savages are spiritual creatures and understand that faith in a higher power (God) grants them serenity and peace.

Develop the habits necessary to become a *Savage*.

Be a *Savage*.

LESSON 7

SAVAGE PROBLEM-SOLVING

When the spring rains came and flooded access to the migratory game animals that fed the tribe, *Savages* would adopt a different plan. After all, possible starvation of their tribe depended on successful hunting. Scouts were sent in both directions of the river to find a narrower crossing. Rafts or canoes were fashioned to take their fellow *Savages* and the tribe to safer ground.

Savages are problem-solvers by nature. While *Peasants* wallow in the circumstance, *Savages* get it done. *Aristocrats* form committees to study the problem.

Savages recognize that in many cases a problem is an opportunity, and they attack the problem with gusto and confidence. Learning to identify the root of the problem at hand is a *Savage* characteristic.

Savages seek the sage advice of their mentors to access wisdom gained earlier from facing adversity. *Savages* never assume *their* answer is the only answer to a problem. But *Savages* realize doing nothing at all could literally cause deaths in their tribe.

Savages keep their wits while others around them may be losing theirs. *Savages* realize there are both short-term and long-term consequences to their actions when it comes to permanently solving a problem. For instance, attacks on their tribe may require a *Savage* to lead his or her tribe on the offensive and eliminate their enemy before they cause damage to the tribe. *Savages* know that weakness invites aggression by their enemies. And the same is true for weaknesses exploited by competitors in business.

There is no such thing as a problem too big for a *Savage*. While *Peasants* look to the *Aristocrats* to solve their problems for them, *Savages* get busy. *Aristocrats* typically lack the critical thinking of a *Savage* and tend to throw money earned by *Savages* at the problem and never address the root cause.

Savages quickly learn from their mistakes and rarely make the same mistake twice. Their survival and that of their tribe depends on it.

Savages maintain a certain pride in their ability to overcome.

Agility and critical thinking are key components of the *Savage* intellect. While *Savages* are viewed by *Aristocrats* as simple-minded, aggressive and unsophisticated, their unique ability to identify, address and solve problems has made *Savages* the most productive individuals in human history.

Learn how to solve problems like a *Savage*.

Be a *Savage*.

LESSON 8

SAVAGE RELATIONSHIPS

*S**avages* develop an inner belief system that is the bedrock of their survival. Part of the inner belief system is to mercilessly protect that inner belief system (attitude) from those that would damage it.

Savages distance themselves from the negative forces that seek to destroy them and/or their dreams—no matter if the negativity is coming from immediate family members or fellow tribesman.

Savages learn there are distinct differences between constructive criticism from a true *Savage* mentor and those of a jealous fellow tribe member who may be envious of the audacity of your choice to break out from *Peasantry* to become the ultimate *Savage* warrior.

Aristocrats are typically universal in their negativity about a *Savage* idea or to a *Savage* who breaks the norms of what is thought of as *accepted* norms. *Savages* stand out from the crowd, even when they don't try to.

There is a natural human attraction to *Savages*. *Savages* are leaders. They are confident. They have a greater purpose to almost everything they do.

Some *Savages* are fortunate enough to have found a mentor—another Savage who has been there and done that. The right mentor is priceless. How does a Savage find a mentor?

Savages look for the traits in a mentor that they want in themselves, not just all the outward trappings of success. The number one rule in finding a mentor is to find someone that has what you want, not just the material trappings, but the lifestyle, attitude, loyalty, persistence and experience that will help you channel your inner *Savage*.

It has always been my experience that a true *Savage* loves to share their gifts with those who seek to be a *Savage*.

For the naysayers that you will certainly experience on your journey to becoming a *Savage*, always ask yourself if the person is dispensing their opinion of your *Savage* pursuit; do they have what you want? If not, they are likely not qualified to lead you to the *Savage* promised land.

Earlier, I stated that "steel sharpens steel." Associate with other *Savages*. Avoid the crab bucket by resisting temptations to lower yourself to the gossip, innuendo and defeatist attitudes of others. Mothers used to teach us, "You are who you associate with." And this is still true today. Yet, many who were taught that lesson surmise that it only applies to children.

It couldn't be truer for an adult in pursuit of becoming a *Savage*.

Throughout human history as Savages have led their tribes, they have also led their families. A true *Savage* is the keeper of their family.

Savages are the patriarchs and matriarchs of their family. A *Savage* sees their responsibility of keeping their family together, intact and supportive of each other. *Savages* set the example in almost every area of their life for their families (and tribes).

This responsibility is the most serious role of the *Savage*, along with being the provider and protector of the family.

Literally, the overall health of the family (and the tribe) depend upon the *Savage*'s ability to lead by example. Every *Savage* has flaws, but the *Savage* will have attributes that far outweigh the flaws, and the family and tribe will know the flaws of the *Savage* but will always weigh them against the *Savage's* attributes.

Savages care about what the family, tribe, fellow *Savages* and mentors think, but they do not waste precious time on those who have no vested interest in the *Savage's* success or the well-being of his family or tribe. And, the *Savage* will have no regard for the opinions of a large number of people. And that's okay.

Savages value the relationships that make their *Savage* pursuit more rewarding!

Be a *Savage*!

LESSON 9

SAVAGE WARFARE

Savages never seek conflict for the sake of conflict, but when faced with their own destruction or that of their tribe, they become *Savage* warriors.

Savages simply win the war.

While *Savages* may lose a skirmish or a specific battle, they regroup, never quit, and are determined to study their adversaries' weaknesses. *War can be a metaphor for competitive business.*

Savages don't fight fair, but they fight with honor. There is nothing fair about warfare. When it becomes the extinction of your tribe versus the distinction of another tribe, there is no decision to be made.

Savages win at all costs.

Savages don't start wars; they finish them, brutally and with extreme force. *Aristocrats* depend on *Savages* to lead and wage *their* wars, leading conscripted *Peasants* to the slaughter like lambs. *Aristocrats*, literally get both *Savages* and *Peasants* killed by following rules of engagement that don't lead to winning. An *Aristocrat* would never lead his tribe in battle, but would issue battle commandments from afar and relegate from safe surroundings.

Savages have an underlying warrior mentality, which can be readily tapped. The *Savage* maintains a controlled 'chip on their shoulder' and taps into that resource when necessary. *Savages* have an uncanny ability to store every slight they've received in life not as baggage but to be used as fuel. Instead of the woe-is-me mentality of the *Peasant*, or the entitled attitude of the *Aristocrat*, the true *Savage* needs very little for motivation. Savages do not depend on the ability to recall an unrelated slight, dig or injustice at any point in their life to fuel the next battle, project, or initiative.

Savages know how effective perception is. A *Savage* that quickly and completely eviscerates his or her opponent in brutal and dominating manner makes the next enemy ponder moving against their tribe. A *Savage* doesn't indiscriminately waste his, hers or their tribe's resources simply for the sake of a battle.

Savages are cunning, and they look at all sides of an argument or conflict before proceeding, but once that die is cast, it is a total commitment to winning.

It has to be. There is no other way for the *Savage*.

Savages plan for contingencies in any scenario. Rarely is a *Savage* caught off guard by an attack from an opponent or a business competitor that is determined to sink them or take their customers.

In the same manner, being keenly aware of the dangerous *Aristocrats,* the *Savages* choose battles carefully. They are fully aware of the power (the government) behind *Aristocrats*. This is why *Savages* cannot afford to ignore or refuse to participate in the significant politics of the day.

Winning is contagious and *Savages* refuse to lose.

While a specific battle may be lost, the *Savage* considers the larger scope of winning the war.

LESSON 10

SAVAGE PERSISTENCE

Savages are stubborn in their *persistence*.

They simply never quit.

Did I say *never*?

Yes, *never!*

This is not to be interpreted as continuing to beat your head against a wall by trying something that has been proven not to work. Persistence is repeated effort to overcome the immediate problem— whether that problem is crossing a wide river to get to the game your tribe needs like your *Savage* ancestors did—or tackling a complex business problem.

Persistence may be the single most important attribute for a *Savage*.

Goal setting is another attribute where *Savages* excel. While any self-help or success book instructs readers to have goals, few couple goal setting with the dogged persistence to achieve.

Yes, *Savages* have written down goals with timelines toward achievement. That *Savage* persistence, however, will keep you on track with your daily habits that are necessary to achieving goals.

Savages dream big and they dream often. Do *Savages* take the time to go see the car, home or boat that he/she can't afford but would love to have?

Goals don't have to be material.

Savages reward themselves when they achieve a goal, but they make the reward commensurate with the goal achieved. The more significant the milestone achieved, the larger the reward!

That dogged *Savage* stubbornness has no room for self-pity, defeatism or whining. And a *Savage* rarely tolerates that from those around him or her.

Failure is never permanent. It is only temporary

for a *Savage*.

Do *Savages* live a charmed life with no catastrophic failures? Rarely. In fact, most highest achieving *Savages* use past failures to catapult them to success. They don't get mired in failure. They lick their wounds, get up, dust themselves off and go to fight another battle.

Defeat is not in the *Savage* vocabulary.

Use your losses as the fuel to your next success!

Savages are optimists. They look at all things as "glass half full." This doesn't mean *Savages* have a Pollyanna view of the world, as a *Savage* is all too aware of the dangers that exist in complacency and naivete.

Stubborn determination in the face of adversity defines a *Savage*. This is especially true when the *Savage* knows deep down in their very being that the strategy, goal or endgame is doable.

Savages are relentless in their quest to *"Hunt it Down, Kill It, and Drag It Home."*

Be a *Savage*!

EPILOGUE

I have been fortunate and blessed to achieve the *Savage* lifestyle. If you would like personal coaching in business or life from the author, David Thomas Roberts, a.k.a. known as the Renegade Capitalist™, please reach directly to me via dtr@defiancepress.com or 281-374-4160. Since I only have 24 hours in a day, my personal consulting service rates are not inexpensive, but I would love to help *you* achieve the status of *"Savage"*!

If you would like to book "The Renegade Capitalist"™ for your next speaking event, please contact us.

Printed in Great Britain
by Amazon